CASES AND COURTROOMS REMEMBERED

Memories of a Texas Trial Lawyer

Larry Funderburk

To Linda, for her love, encouragement, and support....
and to trial lawyers everywhere.

ACKNOWLEDGMENTS

I would like to acknowledge with thanks the invaluable assistance of Mary Ann Dougharty, my wonderful associate, for her advice and editorial expertise, and to Carol Stasky, my faithful secretary, for her help in getting my stories down on paper.

.....because memories fade....

TABLE OF CONTENTS

INTRODUCTION

Clinton Giddings Brown was a well-known San Antonio trial
lawyer. After he retired, he wrote a book entitled "You May
Take the Witness", a wonderfully entertaining book recounting
many of his trials and courtroom experiences. It was published in
1955, and is one of my favorite books. That book was the inspira-
tion for this feeble effort on my part to likewise preserve my memories of trials, courtroom experiences, and hopefully interesting an-
ecdotes from fifty-plus years of trial practice. These accounts are
true, to the best of my memory, although some names have been
changed "to protect the innocent" as they say. However, I have
taken the liberty, from time to time, of supplying details in stories
where my memories of those actual details have faded with time.

One of the great blessings of my life (and I have been fortunate to have enjoyed many) is that my legal career coincided with
a time when jury trials proliferated. The only area of the law
that I ever considered going into was civil trial work. And the
1960's, 70's, 80's and 90's were decades when there were great
opportunities for lawyers interested in trial work. When I gradu-
ated from law school in the fall of 1962, I immediately went on
active duty in the Marine Corps, and after Officer's Basic School,
and Naval Justice School, was assigned duties as a trial/defense
counsel. Those three years in the U. S. Marine Corps afforded

me the opportunity to try many cases, and that is where I began to learn what being a trial lawyer is all about. After my release from active duty at the end of 1965, I joined my older brother's law firm (Funderburk, Murray, and Ramsey, at that time), a small trial firm. I was immediately thrown into the courtroom. I tried my first jury case in my third week with the firm. In those days, it seems as though there were more cases to try than lawyers to try them. I recall that, during my first year, I tried three jury cases in one week. That seems unimaginable now. Of course, they were small cases, involving automobile accidents, but still required the trial lawyer to have basic trial skills, know how to pick a jury, make opening statements, final arguments, examine and cross-examine witnesses, draft the jury charge, etc. These small cases were great for training young lawyers in trial work. In fact, the way lawyers were trained in the trial practice in those days was by trial and error. Young lawyers were simply assigned a case, and thrown into the fray. I cannot recall any formal training programs for trial lawyers in those days. A young, ambitious trial lawyer could try as many cases as he or she had the energy and stamina to try. Cases were simpler to try, because discovery was limited. Many personal injury cases were tried with just a couple of fact witnesses (perhaps the plaintiff and the defendant) and a doctor. Today, every case seemingly becomes a discovery contest, generating documents, objections, motions, and hearings.

Today, civil jury trials are becoming a thing of the past. Lawyers call themselves "litigators" who have never tried a case to a jury. Civil litigation has become a discovery contest. I recently read that civil jury cases in state courts have declined by over 50% between 1992 and 2005. This statistic is from a random sampling by the Bureau of Justice Statistics of state courts in 45 of the 75 most populous U. S. counties. In 1997 there were 3,369 civil jury trials in Texas state courts; yet in 2012, there were fewer than 1,200.

I'm sure there are many reasons for the decline of the civil jury trial, but I think one of the major reasons is that trial work is hard work. Clinton Giddings Brown, in his book "You May Take the Witness" says "...there is nothing to being a trial lawyer except hard work and some knowledge of human nature....". He is certainly right about the "hard work" part. I cannot imagine any endeavor more difficult than trying a hard-fought case to a jury.

Vic Hall was a part time professor at Baylor Law School, and I was in his criminal law class. He often reminded his students that "the law is a jealous mistress". I don't remember much about criminal law from his course, but I sure remember how he tried to impress upon his students that in order to succeed in the practice of law, one had to work extremely hard, and extraordinarily long hours. He talked about the necessity to work on Saturdays and Sundays in order to be a successful trial lawyer. At the time, as a first year law student, I thought he must be exaggerating, or simply trying to weed out those who did not have an inclination for hard work. I think most of my fellow students thought he was exaggerating, as well. In the years since, I have learned that he was exactly right, and was not exaggerating at all. I believe that trial work, if practiced as it should be practiced, is among the most strenuous of all occupations or professions. The trial of a lawsuit is extremely hard work. Prodigious preparation is required. I found that throughout my career of trying cases, weekend work and after hours work was required. Most young lawyers today, coming into the profession, don't seem to understand and appreciate the commitment necessary, and many are unprepared for the challenge of trying lawsuits.

When I was discharged from the Marine Corps, and returned to Texas to begin my law practice, I interviewed for a job with Rex Houston, a legendary East Texas trial lawyer. His firm was Wellborn and Houston, in Henderson, Texas. My appointment with him was scheduled for the middle of a weekday afternoon.

When I arrived at his office for the interview, his secretary advised me that he was in trial, in the Rusk County Courthouse, across the street from his office. She suggested that I go to the courtroom and observe the trial for the remainder of the afternoon, and that Mr. Houston would visit with me when the trial recessed for the day. I did as she suggested. When the judge recessed the trial for the day, I introduced myself to Rex, and we walked back to his office and visited for a considerable amount of time. This was in December of 1965. Rex told me that he had already tried close to 50 cases during that calendar year. This would have amounted to almost a case per week during that year. I do not believe he was exaggerating. I remember very well that he related to me his schedule for a typical week. He said that he was usually in trial from Monday morning through Thursday or Friday. On Saturday, he "cleaned up his desk", attending to all the matters that had come to his attention throughout the week. On Sunday, he prepared for the coming week's trial. I was duly impressed! Such was the life of a busy trial lawyer in the mid-1960's. I could not have begun my career as a young, eager, trial lawyer at a more opportune time. I have tried over 150 cases to a jury verdict. Lawyers starting out today will never have such a golden opportunity as I was fortunate enough to have. It has been a wonderful career.

What follows is not in any particular chronological order, or in any order, for that matter. It simply is my recollection of cases that I have tried or otherwise participated in, and which may have some appeal to the reader. Come to think of it, I can't imagine why any of these stories and vignettes would be of much interest to anyone who did not participate in them. Nevertheless, here they are.

CHAPTER 1

THE NACOGDOCHES
INSURANCE AGENT

I spent five years in Longview, trying cases throughout East
and Northeast Texas. These were primarily automobile accident cases and worker's compensation cases. I had not been in
Longview very long when I was called to trial in an automobile
accident case. The accident occurred in downtown Nacogdoches.
The plaintiff brought suit against two defendants. The plaintiff's
attorney was a well-known trial lawyer, but who had a somewhat
tarnished reputation. At the conclusion of the trial, I was to learn
why his reputation was less than sterling. I represented one of the
defendants, and a prominent defense lawyer from Lufkin, Kenzie
Hallmark, represented the other defendant. Kenzie and I were
not at all adverse to each other; both of us blamed the accident
on the plaintiff. After voir dire examination of the jury panel,
Kenzie and I "struck together". In other words, we collaborated
on striking the jury. One of the potential jurors was a prominent citizen of Nacogdoches, an insurance agent, named Joe Max
Green. He would seem to be an ideal defendant's juror. In fact,
he and Kenzie were good friends, and Kenzie's partner played golf

with him most Saturdays. We both felt that the plaintiff's attorney would strike him. When the jury was seated, what a surprise when he was seated as a juror! Why would the plaintiff's attorney leave an obvious defense juror on the jury? As the trial moved along, I began to be quite concerned as I slowly came to the realization that I was the only party to the case who did not have some connection with juror Green. It was logical to assume that he and the plaintiff's attorney were at least acquainted since they were both businessmen in Nacogdoches, and I knew that he and Kenzie were friends. I was the only one who had no relationship to Joe Max! And, I came to learn during the trial that the plaintiff's attorney placed all of his insurance with agent Green. By the time the trial was finished, I had convinced myself that Joe Max was going to be the foreman of the jury, and I was about to be ambushed, as the only outsider in the case.

What a relief when the verdict was announced! The jury exonerated my client, placed some negligence on Kenzie's client, but placed most of the fault on the plaintiff. Joe Max Green sought me out immediately after the jury was dismissed and related to me that he was, indeed, the plaintiff's attorney's insurance agent, and that on the Friday before the trial started on Monday, the plaintiff's attorney had come to his office and increased his coverages and purchased additional insurance coverage. The panel of veniremen had been published in the district clerk's office that day. He went on to say that he fully expected the plaintiff's attorney to be in his office when he returned to move his insurance portfolio to another agent.

Thank the Lord for honest and courageous jurors!

CHAPTER 2

THE COURTROOM DEMONSTRATION
THAT ALMOST BACK-FIRED

The case was filed in Robertson County (aka "Booger County") Texas. The county seat is Franklin. The county is an economically deprived, mostly rural, central Texas county. The plaintiff, Richard Boyd, was represented by Mac Gann, a wonderful trial lawyer, and a good friend. He spoke the language of Booger County, and was right at home there, although he was based in Houston. Mac was colorful, down to earth, and his specialty was trying cases in "the country" because he really connected with rural jurors.

I represented Werner Ladders, the largest manufacturer of aluminum and fiberglass ladders in the world. The hardware store in Hearne where the ladder was purchased was represented by Bob Burleson, a very fine trial lawyer from Temple. The case involved a 10 foot aluminum stepladder. The ladder was in the courtroom. The right side-rail was bent inward, toward the center of the ladder, below the knee brace. It was still capable of remaining upright, and supporting a load, although it was unstable or "wobbly". The allegation was that Boyd was on the ladder, and the side-rail just bent, or buckled, causing him to fall, sustaining serious injuries. According to the plaintiff's allegations, the ladder was under-designed, weak, and failed to meet its 250 pound duty rating. Our defense was that the ladder was not defective, was strong, and had been tested to four times its duty rating. We contended that the accident occurred due to the negligence of Boyd in extending his body outside the side-rails, losing his balance, causing the ladder to tip over and fall, and that the bend or "buckling" occurred when he fell on top of the ladder.

Werner sent one of their staff engineers to act as Werner's representative at trial, and to offer expert testimony about the manufacture of the ladder, the testing thereof, and the strength of the ladder. Although I had tried several cases for Werner previously, this was the first time I had met this particular engineer; he was new to Werner, and to me. At the beginning of the trial, he told me how we were going to demonstrate the strength of this particular model of ladder; he said that we would bring a new ladder, same model, identical to the incident ladder, and we would, in the presence of the jury, saw both knee braces in two, and saw one side-rail halfway through. Then, we would have four people get on the ladder. My response was "no, no, no.....we're not going to attempt such a stunt; if something were to go wrong, the result would be disastrous". But the young engineer would not take no for an answer. He insisted that the demonstration would work, and would be very convincing. He said that if we lost the case, he could not go back to Werner and tell them that the demonstration had not been utilized. He assured me that he knew what he was doing, and that the demonstration would be successful. His insistence finally prevailed, and against my better judgment, I consented to the demonstration.

The plaintiff rested his case on Friday afternoon. The defense was to begin its presentation on Monday morning. On Saturday, the engineer purchased a step-ladder, identical to the ladder in question. He also purchased a hack saw, and a sheet of plywood to put the ladder on, so that we did not damage or scuff the courtroom's hardwood floor. Outside the presence of the jury, we informed the judge, Judge Bartlett, what we proposed to do. Mac said he had no objection. I think he knew that the judge would probably permit it, whether he objected or not, but more importantly, I think he believed that our proposed demonstration was not going to be successful and the demonstration would back-fire.

To say that we got the attention of the jury would be an understatement. The jury was leaning forward in their seats as the young engineer sawed both knee braces in two, and sawed half way through the right side-rail. Then Bob Burleson (who weighed about 250 pounds) climbed to the top of the ladder. Next, the engineer got on the ladder. Then the court reporter mounted the ladder. And finally, I stood on the bottom rung. My heart was pounding; I realized what a chance we were taking. I looked down at the side-rail which had been sawed half way through, and I could see the side-rail bending back and forth. You could hear a pin drop as the four of us stood on the ladder. Finally Mac broke the silence, and relieved the tension when he said "Now can I get on the ladder?"

Thankfully, we all removed ourselves from the ladder without the ladder collapsing, and we won the case. I still cannot believe that I permitted the demonstration. I did so only at the insistence of the engineer who was sent by my client to represent it at trial. I do not recommend such demonstrations. I believe that we were very fortunate that the ladder did not collapse.

One final note about the case. As I have already mentioned, the plaintiff's ladder was in the courtroom. It had a bent side-rail, and was "wobbly", but would still support weight. Bob Burleson, who represented the hardware store in Hearne where the ladder was purchased, delivered his closing argument while sitting on the top of the ladder. Bob was a fine trial lawyer, and a very colorful one.

CHAPTER 3

THE FUSE THAT BLEW UP DOW CHEMICAL OR HELLO MARY CARTER

A "Mary Carter" agreement is defined as a settlement with one or more defendants, whereby the settling defendant retains a financial interest in the case. In other words, in a case where there are multiple defendants, the plaintiff settles with one or more of the defendants, but the defendants who settle remain in the case, with the agreement that they share in the plaintiff's recovery against the non-settling defendant or defendants. Usually, the agreement includes a provision that the settling defendant(s) must actively participate in the trial and assist the plaintiff in seeking a recovery against the non-settling defendant. Of course, the jury is never told of this arrangement. The agreement greatly improves the chances that the plaintiff will win the case, and the settling defendant (s) has an excellent chance, normally, to recover all or part of the settlement he has made with the plaintiff. The name, "Mary Carter", comes from a 1976 Florida case in which Mary Carter Paint Company was a defendant and such an agreement was used against it. "Mary Carter" agreements have now been declared void in Texas as against public policy, but in the late

70's and 80's, they were frequently used in civil cases with more than one defendant. They were particularly pernicious. These arrangements skewed the natural positions of the parties. They turned defendants against each other; they allowed the plaintiff and the settling defendant (s) to "gang up" on the non-settling defendant and even caused the settling defendant (s) to agree with the plaintiff as to the damages that should be awarded. And they were very effective in causing large verdicts to be awarded against the party who did not settle.

I found myself the victim of such an agreement in the case of *Colvin v. Federal Pacific Electric Company*. The case was filed in Brazoria County, Texas, a county well-known for its propensity for large plaintiff's verdicts. The plaintiffs were represented by Mike Gallagher, an outstanding trial lawyer from Houston. My client was Federal Pacific Electric Company, which manufactured industrial electrical equipment. The product in question was a small fuse, manufactured by Federal Pacific, and used as a component in a chemical process at the Dow Chemical plant in Freeport, a huge industrial complex. The event which gave rise to the lawsuit was a devastating explosion which resulted in the death of Emmett Colvin, and severe burns and other injuries to several other Dow employees. Gallagher brought suit against several defendants, including my client, and including Dow Chemical, among others, for gross negligence. An engineer, employed by Dow, as part of the investigation into the cause of the explosion, opined that the Federal Pacific fuse was defectively manufactured, and because of the alleged defect, it opened (broke the circuit) prematurely. In other words, he claimed that the fuse should have maintained circuit continuity at the voltage level to which it was exposed, but failed to do so, opening instead, which set in motion a series of events which caused the explosion.

My position was rather simple. A fuse is *designed* to open, thereby breaking an electrical circuit. Everyone knows that such is the purpose and function of a fuse. The problem which led to the explosion was the design of the process, which produced an explosion when a circuit was interrupted. My client manufactured and sold the fuse, but had no input nor knowledge of the application of the fuse. Dow designed the process. Other defendants in the case participated in the design of the process. I argued that my client's fuse did exactly what it was designed to do - open and break the circuit. If it had failed to open, allowing excess current to flow, there might be an argument that it was defectively designed or manufactured. But in this case, the premature opening, if, indeed, it was premature, was not the cause of the explosion.

Before trial, the Colvin family settled with all the defendants, except my client, on the basis of a "Mary Carter" agreement. This meant that they all cooperated with the plaintiffs, and argued that my client was solely responsible for the death of Emmett Colvin and the injuries to other Dow employees. At trial, I found myself at one counsel table, and lawyers for all the settling parties, along with the plaintiff's attorneys, at the other counsel table. The battle lines were clearly drawn. My local counsel was Jim Bradford, a wonderful resource throughout the trial. Jim was an Angleton attorney, well-known throughout Brazoria County, who described himself as a small town country lawyer. But he was invaluable in helping to select the jury, and in offering advice and counsel throughout the two and one half week trial. I was also assisted at trial by Dwayne Newton, a young lawyer at the time, who was assisting in one of his first cases. He did an outstanding job.

My client representative was Harry Droullard, from Cleveland, Ohio. He was in attendance throughout the trial, and was taken aback at the Texas civil justice system which allowed such practices as the "Mary Carter" agreement. He frankly did not believe that we could win the case under the circumstances we had to deal with. I carried an old, beaten up brief case. Harry promised to buy me a new brief case if we won the case - never believing he would have to carry through on his promise. By the way, I am still waiting for my new brief case.

Much to every one's surprise, we won the case. The jury placed 100% of the fault on Dow Chemical, and none on Federal Pacific, or on the other settling defendants. The jury was able to see through the arguments of the plaintiffs and Dow, and determined that the cause of the explosion was the design of the process, and not the fuse.

Several aspects of the trial stand out in my mind. We had hired an expert on process design. He seemed to be well qualified, but he was a novice at giving testimony and serving as an expert witness. When his deposition was taken before trial, he was extremely critical of Emmett Colvin himself, and even went so far as to say that if Colvin had not perished in the explosion, he would have probably been fired by Dow because of his negligence. His attitude and demeanor were confrontational and angry, and I was very reluctant to put him on the stand. On the other hand, if we did not put him on the stand, the plaintiff would show his video deposition to the jury, without an opportunity for him to explain his unfortunate criticism of Colvin. We decided to put him on. Jim Bradford spent an entire day working with him in an attempt to calm him down and soften his attitude. When he was called as a witness, he was asked about his criticism of Colvin, as expressed in his deposition. He turned to the Colvin family, and confessed that he was wrong to blame the explosion on Mr. Colvin, and sought their forgiveness for his unfortunate remarks at his deposition. He was humble and contrite, and he turned out to be a very credible witness. His testimony may have been the turning point in the case. Jim Bradford was responsible for changing his attitude. Charlie Lyman, the attorney for Dow, and a very good trial lawyer, was heard to remark, "How do you cross-examine Santa Claus?"

One of the plaintiff's expert witnesses was a gentleman who had an extensive history of testifying in product liability cases. We researched him thoroughly, obtaining numerous depositions he had given, and were able to identify over 100 different products that he had testified about, and offering the opinions that each of such products was defective. The jury leaned forward in their chairs, and focused their attention on him, as we asked him about each of the products that he had condemned as being defective. The list seemed to go on and on. It must have taken an hour or so to go through the list. By the time we were finished with our cross-examination, he had been fully discredited.

Our primary electrical expert witness was Ron Rhoten, a professor of electrical engineering at Oklahoma State University in Stillwater, Oklahoma. He almost did not make it to the trial. He was scheduled to testify on Monday morning of the second week of trial. I had asked him to bring with him several industrial fuses of different designs and configurations for demonstration purposes. He carried these fuses in his brief case. He flew from Oklahoma City on Sunday afternoon, and was required to change planes in Dallas. The plan was that I would meet him in Houston, and drive him to Angleton. But as he attempted to board the flight from Dallas, he was detained, escorted to a room, where he was questioned about the fuses in his brief case. He missed his connecting flight to Houston, and it appeared as though he would not be able to board any flight to Houston with his brief case of fuses. Apparently, it was thought that the fuses may have been bomb-making devices, or weapons of some kind. Finally, a supervisor was called, who quickly identified the fuses correctly as simple industrial fuses, which presented no threat to safety. Ron was able to catch a later flight, and finally arrived in Houston late Sunday night. Needless to say, I was greatly relieved when he finally arrived.

Several years ago, I was in Jim Bradford's office. On the wall of his reception area, there hung a glass-enclosed case containing the fuse.....with a caption that read "THE FUSE THAT BLEW UP DOW CHEMICAL".

CHAPTER 4

A 'FIRED-UP' ATTORNEY

Henry Giessel is a court-house legend. He has probably tried more cases than any lawyer in Houston, and has won most of them. One of his more memorable cases was *Arthur Lee Howard v. Faberge*. Arthur Lee Howard was sixteen years old. As he left home for a date with his girl-friend, he was wearing a polyester shirt or jersey, and he splashed on a copious amount of Brut 33 Splash On Lotion. The Brut lotion was a Faberge product. Then he lit a cigarette, and dropped the lighted match into his waistband. He immediately went up in flames, sustaining severe burns to his chest, upper arms, and face. His lawsuit complained that neither the shirt nor the lotion carried any warning about flammability. He was represented by Wayne Fisher, a well-known and very talented trial lawyer. Faberge was represented by Henry Giessel, and I represented the manufacturer of the shirt. My client settled before trial, and the case proceeded to trial against Faberge. Faberge disputed the plaintiff's claims that Brut was flammable.

During Henry's final argument, or summation, he suddenly produced a bottle of Brut, and standing before the jury, he poured the contents on his arm, and lit a match, passing it over the doused arm. He then said "I don't think Mr. Howard could put on a shirt any faster than I can light a match. Let's see how he did it." Then he said "God, if I am wrong, burn me." He went on to urge the jury to try the same experiment at home to prove that the lotion is not flammable.

Of course, he did not set himself on fire. But to the incredulous jurors, it appeared that he risked burning himself up before the devil even had a chance at him.

Not surprisingly, the jury exonerated Faberge, but the plaintiff appealed the verdict. The appellate court was not amused. It held that the attempt to ignite the substance on Henry's arm amounted to "an unauthorized in-court experiment...with an unidentified liquid...". The jury's verdict was overturned, and the case was remanded to the trial court for a new trial.

Sometimes trial lawyers can be <u>too</u> creative.

CHAPTER 5

THE BANDIDOS CASE

Jorge Diaz was a member of the Bandidos, the motorcycle gang, and he looked every bit the part with his long hair, tattoos, bandana, black leather jacket and boots. Eric Fischer was an employee of a contractor who was working on the premises of a plant in Pasadena owned and operated by ICI Americas. My client was Mundy Contractors, also working on the premises of ICI Americas. One of Mundy's jobs was to provide security for the plant, and to provide security guards at the front gate to the plant. Fischer reported to work at 7:00 a.m., in a drunken state. His intoxication was obvious to everyone who encountered him on that fateful morning. The Mundy guard on the front gate instructed him to go to the contractor's locker room, and to stay there. He was told not to try to report for work within the plant. When he got to the contractor's locker room, he was again told by a supervisor to stay in the locker room until he sobered up. Nevertheless, he decided to go home, went to his car, drove out of the plant, and caused the accident which took the life of Jorge Diaz, the Bandido. Fischer lost control of his automobile on a curve, crossed the center stripe, and hit Diaz's motorcycle head-on. Diaz was killed instantly.

Three different women filed suit, each claiming to be Diaz's common-law wife. Several children also were made parties to the case since it was claimed that they were children of Diaz, although he had never recognized them as his children. One could not imagine a more undesirable image to present to a jury. However, he was entirely blameless in causing the accident in which he was killed. The case proceeded to a three week trial. At the conclusion of the plaintiff's case, my client, Mundy, was granted an instructed verdict, and was dismissed from the case. The case proceeded as to the remaining defendants, and was settled prior to the verdict.

The aspects of the case which stand out in my mind are the claims of the three women, each of whom claimed to be his wife, and the photographs of his "family" - the Bandidos. The dispute among the three women as to who was the surviving spouse over-shadowed the dispute as to liability for the fatal accident. Several photographs of Diaz with the Bandidos made their way into evidence, and they were very interesting, to say the least.

There was never a dull moment in the trial of this case.

CHAPTER 6

DID HE REALLY SAY THAT?

The most important witness in any personal injury case is the plaintiff himself or herself. I have always believed that the plaintiff is Exhibit # 1. If the plaintiff is articulate, humble, and presents a good appearance, those attributes will go a long way toward a favorable verdict for the plaintiff. On the other hand, if the plaintiff makes a poor appearance, or is arrogant, or appears to be malingering or exaggerating his injuries, he will have a hard time securing a favorable verdict. And, it is surprising how one wrong answer can turn a case around.

Such was the case in *Scot Bias v. Hoechst Celanese Corporation,* tried in Judge Mark Davidson's Eleventh Judicial District Court.

Scot Bias was a young man employed by a contractor in the Hoechst Celanese chemical plant. He was an experienced pipefitter. The case involved an alleged electrical shock, causing Bias to fall from a pipe rack and become suspended in his safety harness. His damages were significant. He had two surgeries, one to his neck and one to his shoulder. His lawyer sought more than a half million dollars.

The case went well for the plaintiff, until one question was put to him on cross-examination, and his answer to the question.

His doctors had given him a medical clearance to return to work on a limited basis several months before trial, but he had failed to return. There was no apparent reason for his failure. So, on cross-examination, I asked him, "Mr. Bias, what are your intentions about returning to the work-force? When this trial is over, do you intend to go back to work?" There was a long pause, and then he replied, "Well, if this jury doesn't give me any money, I guess I will have to."

It was almost as if you could sense that his case had been lost. The jury sat back in their chairs, and appeared to lose interest in the rest of his testimony. His counsel told me later that he wanted to crawl under the counsel table.

The verdict was for the defendant. A simple question, and an unfortunate (for him) answer, turned the case around.

CHAPTER 7

THE WRENCH WITH
THE BENT HANDLE

Sometimes cases are won or lost for reasons that entirely escape the lawyers and the experts. We attorneys believe that we know what evidence will persuade a jury, and what the key factors are that will control the verdict. And sometimes we can be entirely wrong; a jury will sometimes seize upon some fact or some piece of evidence which will decide the case, and which the attorneys and experts have not even considered.

That's what happened in the case of *Joe Garcia v. Danaher Corporation*.

Joe Garcia was a long time employee of Dow Chemical and an experienced pipe-fitter. He was using a ratchet wrench to tighten nuts on a bolt, to secure a flange. As he pulled on the handle of the wrench, the ratchet mechanism failed, causing Garcia to fall backwards, and into a protective rail, resulting in a serious back injury. The wrench was manufactured by my client, The Danaher Corporation. The lawsuit which resulted was filed in Brazoria County, Texas. It was alleged that the wrench was defectively manufactured or designed, in that the ratcheting mechanism failed to withstand the load or force which Garcia applied. If that were true, the wrench was defective, since it obviously should be designed to withstand the torque that a man could generate.

Our defense was that some additional force or load was placed on the wrench, which was beyond the capability of the wrench to withstand. A common practice with plant maintenance workers, although illegal, is the use of a "cheater bar" or "cheater pipe". This practice involves inserting the handle of the wrench into a pipe, thereby extending the length of the handle, and increasing the torque. The result is that sometimes more torque is applied than the wrench is designed to withstand. Our expert's examination of the wrench revealed a small mark on the handle of the wrench which he believed represented evidence that a "cheater pipe" had been used to over-torque the wrench. OSHA and other safety organizations have condemned the use of "cheaters", for exactly this reason. They allow a worker to apply too much torque, exceeding the capability of the wrench to withstand it. Of course, Garcia denied the use of a "cheater". Our expert also offered the opinion that the wrench may have been over-torqued on some prior occasion, and the mechanism may have been compromised and weakened as a result.

The wrench in question was in the courtroom, and was admitted into evidence. It was passed to the jury, and examined by all 12 jurors. Our expert had thoroughly examined the wrench, as had the plaintiff's expert. And, the attorneys and parties to the case had handled the wrench over and over, both before and during the trial. None of us noted anything unusual about the wrench, other than the broken ratchet mechanism.

This was a hard-fought case, and we were in trial about a week. The jury retired to consider their verdict. After two hours, the jury had its verdict. The jury found that the wrench was not defective, and the verdict was for the defense.

The next morning, I was in my office, when I received a call from the foreman of the jury. What he told me was quite a surprise. The wrench in question was in the jury room with the jurors, and with the other evidence in the case. As the jurors were examining the wrench, one of the jurors rolled the handle across the table in the jury room. As he did so, another juror noticed that it did not roll smoothly as you would expect a perfectly round handle to do; rather, each revolution of the handle produced an indication that the handle was not straight. The handle was bent! This was clearly proof that the wrench had been over-torqued.

There is no telling how many times the wrench had been examined before and during trial, by myself, my associates, opposing counsel, the experts for both sides, and others. No one had noticed that the handle of the wrench was bent. It took the jury to discover the most important evidence in the case.

So much for the careful preparation by the lawyers and the experts; the jury figured the case out by itself!

CHAPTER 8

THE SOCIALIST PARTY PLAINTIFF

The case of *Evelyn Sell, et al v. Volkswagen, et al* was an interesting case for several reasons. The case was tried before the Honorable Ruby Sondock, an outstanding trial judge, who went on to become the first woman to serve on the Supreme Court of Texas. I had the privilege of trying several cases before Judge Sondock. I was also privileged to work with some outstanding trial lawyers. Sidney Ravkind of Houston, and Jim Tuck of Detroit, Michigan, represented the plaintiffs. Gay Brinson, Gerald Coley, Frank Bean and I represented the defendants.

Evelyn Sell, her son Eric Sell, and Katharine Stallworth were traveling from Oberlin, Ohio, to Houston, when the 1971 Volkswagen in which they were traveling blew a tire, went out of control, and crashed near Memphis, Tennessee. Mrs. Sell was left a paraplegic. Eric suffered serious brain damage, and Miss Stallworth sustained a broken hip. They were returning from a Socialist Workers Party convention. They contended at trial that the blow-out was due to improper camber (misalignment) wear of the tire and that the defendants were negligent in failing to inspect and test the vehicle, and in breaching express and implied warranties that the vehicle was safe for normal use, and would continue to be safe if serviced in accordance with the prescribed maintenance program. The car had been purchased from C. B. Smith Volkswagen, and had been serviced by both C. B. Smith Volkswagen and Mel Croan Volkswagen. I represented C. B. Smith Volkswagen.

The most interesting aspect of the case revolved around Evelyn Sell's membership in the Socialist Workers Party and her attorney's efforts to keep the jury from learning of her party affiliation, and her political beliefs. Sidney Ravkind, in his voir dire examination of the jury panel, stated that the evidence would show that Evelyn Sell was very active in politics and then asked if anyone on the jury panel would hold it against her if the evidence showed that she had assisted "in organizing" and "that sort of thing." When one member of the panel asked "What kind, I mean for our government or against our government?", Sidney replied, "....for our government, I can assure you....but we don't want to get into parties is really what the problem is, I suppose."

While the plaintiff's political affiliation ordinarily would not be relevant, Judge Sondock ruled that the plaintiff's attorney had "opened the door" and that the defendants were entitled to offer evidence about her political beliefs, the purpose of the trip, etc. We also debated, outside the presence of the jury, whether the Socialist Workers Party is "for our government or against our government". I recall that Gay Brinson secured a copy of the Socialist Workers Party platform, and we all studied it carefully as we debated the issue. What a strange issue to dominate the trial of an automobile accident case!

The jury's verdict was for the defendants, and it stood up on appeal. Sometimes cases can take strange twists and turns. This one surely did.

As an aside, Jim Tuck, a brilliant trial lawyer, was killed in the 1987 crash of a Northwest Airlines plane, on a flight from Detroit to Phoenix. He was 45 years old.

CHAPTER 9

A STRONG JUROR

Iva Pearl Thompson was a widow who lived in a double-wide on Farm Road 2419 in south Anderson County with her eleven year old daughter, Judy. Judy was the light of her life, a beautiful little girl, smart, helpful and all that a mother could hope for in a daughter. It was almost dusk on a summer Sunday evening. Judy was riding her bicycle near her home, on or near the narrow two-lane farm road. She was on her way home, riding her bicycle in a westerly direction. Ruth Motley, a prominent citizen of Palestine, was traveling west in her automobile along the same stretch of road. She was on her way home, having spent the afternoon at the Pine Lodge Club, near Elkhart. She would later testify that she had consumed two drinks, but she was not impaired. For whatever reason, Ms. Motley never saw Judy before striking her. Judy died instantly as a result of the accident. Perhaps the sun was in each of their eyes as they traveled west at dusk. The question was whether Judy was on the paved portion of the roadway, or on the shoulder. Motley claimed that Judy had to be on the roadway, because she (Motley) never left the paved portion of the roadway. The only eye-witness was Tommy Harrison, who witnessed the accident in his rear-view mirror. He had been traveling west, ahead of Motley.

He would testify that Judy was on the shoulder of the roadway at the time of the collision.

My brother, Weldon, and I represented Iva Pearl Thompson in her suit for damages against Ruth Motley. The case was tried in the Third Judicial District Court of Anderson County in 1967. I had not been practicing law very long. This was the first case I had the privilege of trying in that large, historic old courtroom. I was later privileged to try several more cases there. As a young boy, I made my way into a packed courtroom to watch Percy Foreman defend a murder case there.

In 1967, recovery for the death of a minor was limited to monetary or pecuniary damages. In other words, Iva Pearl was not entitled to recover damages for grief, sorrow, loss of companionship, mental anguish, etc. for the wrongful death of her daughter; she was limited to her monetary loss. The law has since been changed; now, a parent is entitled to damages for mental anguish, loss of companionship, sorrow, etc. This really amounted to a legal fiction. It would be almost impossible to show that she suffered a monetary loss. Any parent knows that a child, in most cases, from a purely monetary standpoint, is a liability, not a source of financial gain. In addition, Ms. Motley's liability insurance was limited to $25,000, so that was the maximum that we had any hope of recovering, even if we could prove monetary damages.

Ms. Motley was a physical education teacher at the Junior High School in Palestine. She had a somewhat controversial reputation because she taught "folk dancing" to her junior high school students, and led an elaborate production each spring, known as the Folk Festival. Many in the community did not believe that "folk dancing" was an appropriate subject for junior high school students. Ms. Motley passed away before trial, but after her deposition was taken. The case continued against her estate.

The Motley estate was represented by Tim Kelly of Dallas, a highly experienced and skilled trial lawyer. The judge, the

Honorable Wayne Lawrence, was quick to remind Weldon and me, at the beginning of the trial, that Kelly had tried a number of cases in his court, and had never lost one. But we had no choice, except to try the case, since Kelly and the insurance company never made a settlement offer.

The cast of characters was interesting. I grew up in Palestine. My parents lived there. My family was always active in the First Baptist Church. Judge Lawrence was one of the stalwart church leaders in the First Baptist Church. The foreperson of the jury turned out to be Mrs. Andrew Overton, also a very active and strong church leader in the First Baptist Church.

Jury selection was rather routine until we came to Mrs. Overton. She answered questions from the attorneys to the effect that she was acquainted with Ms. Motley, but she could be fair and base her verdict on the evidence. The conventional wisdom was that we should exercise a peremptory strike on her, because of her acquaintance with Motley. We really struggled with that decision. I had a "gut feeling", however, that we should leave her on the jury; she was a strong-minded woman whose values might have been at odds with Motley's values. While the two women were acquainted, I doubted they were close. They might even be seen as rivals. So, we decided to take the risk; we left her on the jury. We were sure that Kelly would not strike her, since she would ordinarily be thought of as a defense-minded juror. Sure enough, she ended up on the jury, and was elected foreperson of the jury.

In 1967, the contributory negligence of a plaintiff, or plaintiff's decedent, was a complete defense. The court instructed the jury that Judy's conduct was to be judged by that of an ordinarily prudent child of eleven years of age. Also, in 1967, the court submitted jury questions about every act or omission of a party which was pled, and on which there was evidence. Tim Kelly had pled numerous acts which he contended amounted to negligence on the part of Judy. Judge Lawrence submitted each one to the jury.

When the court's charge was finally put together, it contained fifty special issues, or jury questions. My heart sank; it would seem to be impossible for the jury to answer fifty special issues, most of them inquiring about Judy's conduct, without finding some fault or negligence on the part of Judy. We were about ready to pack it in, and concede the case to the defendant. What a shock, when the buzzer sounded from the jury room in just 45 minutes! The jury had a verdict! Mrs. Overton was the foreperson. The jury had gone through 50 special issues in only 45 minutes, and had answered every one in the plaintiff's favor. Damages were found to be $35,000. We had called as a witness the principal of Judy's school who testified that she was bright, helpful, and could reasonably be expected, based upon his experience and expertise, to go to college and be of financial assistance to her mother in the future. At the time, 1967, this was thought to be the largest verdict ever reported in Texas for the death of a minor child (How times have changed!). I believe that Mrs. Overton was almost single-handedly responsible for the verdict.

It has often been said that jury selection is the most important phase of a jury case and that the case will usually be decided based on who is left on the jury. That was certainly true in the case of *Thompson v. Motley*. Mrs. Overton plowed through 50 special issues in 45 minutes and the rest of the jurors followed.

A strong woman, indeed!

CHAPTER 10

SOUTH TEXAS: A WORLD OF ITS OWN

The trial of the case of *Melchor Gutierrez, Sr., and Petra Gutierrez, Individually and as Representatives of the Estate of Melchor Gutierrez, Jr. and Juan Martinez v. Precision Orchard Services* was not a pleasant experience for me. The case involved the collision of a car and a tractor on a farm to market road. The issue in the case was which vehicle crossed the center-stripe, into the path of the other. The collision occurred at 7:00 a.m. The car was occupied by the plaintiff, Juan Martinez, who was driving, and Melchor Gutierrez, Jr., a passenger, who was killed in the collision. I represented the owner of the tractor, Precision Orchard Services, and their employee, who was driving the tractor. Juan Martinez, the driver of the automobile, was charged with negligent homicide. I requested his deposition, but his attorneys resisted, because of the criminal charges, and stated that he would have to claim his 5th Amendment right to refuse to testify. Strangely, the district attorney's office in Hidalgo County did not seem to be interested in setting the criminal case for trial. On the other hand, the plaintiffs' attorneys in the civil case aggressively pursued their case. The trial judge was Judge Aida Salinas-Flores. She, of course, sustained the plaintiffs' motion for protection, and I was not allowed to depose the driver of the vehicle, although a trial date was imminent.

The case was set for trial on a Monday in August in Hidalgo County. The parties were notified to appear on the previous Friday for a pretrial conference, and presentation of all pending motions, including my motion to be permitted to depose Juan Lopez. My contention was that I was being denied due process of law, if I were forced to go to trial without the deposition of the driver of the adverse vehicle, and the most important witness in the case. I also argued that the case on the merits should be continued; the deposition of Martinez, if taken at this late date, would likely provide information to be investigated and analyzed, and there simply was not time for that to occur. The judge ruled that I could take the deposition of Martinez the following morning, Saturday, but she would not continue the case. She ordered the parties to mediate the case on Monday morning, and if the mediation was unsuccessful, we would begin the trial of the case on Tuesday morning. The mediation was unsuccessful. So we really had only the weekend to prepare for trial with the benefit of Martinez's deposition.

The trial of the case lasted about two weeks. Fortunately, I was able to negotiate a "high-low" agreement during trial. The agreement was that, regardless of the jury's verdict, the damages would be capped at $2 million, and the defendant would be required to pay $350,000, even if the defendant was exonerated, or the damages were found to be less than $350,000. This was important, because my client's liability insurance coverage was limited to $2 million. A verdict in excess of that figure could very well wipe out the company. The jury returned a verdict of about $2.5 million.

I prepared the judgment in the case. Court costs were to be taxed against the party incurring same, including the cost of the experts. This was clearly stated in the judgment which I prepared. Several experts had testified in the case, including some expensive computer animations. So court costs were significant. I sent the judgment to the lead attorney for the plaintiffs for his approval and signature, before sending it to the court for entry. When it came back to me, the judgment had been changed, charging all court costs to the defendant. If I had not reviewed the judgment carefully when the plaintiffs' attorney sent it back to me, I would have missed this change. Even the "footie", the initials of the preparer at the bottom of the page had been made to appear that my office was the preparer of the changed document! I promptly called the plaintiffs' attorney, who claimed ignorance of the whole affair. I re-drafted the judgment providing that court costs are being taxed against the party incurring same. This time, I sent the judgment to my local counsel, Juan Gonzales, who personally delivered it to Judge Salinas-Flores, and requested that she sign it in his presence, which she did.

South Texas: Another world!

CHAPTER 11

O BROTHER WHERE ART THOU

David Roberts was a boilermaker/pipefitter who worked for a contractor in a chemical plant near Houston. He was working on a small platform, high up in a structure. A huge crane was positioned nearby. The counterweight on the crane resembled a wrecking ball. The operator of the crane allowed the counterweight to slowly descend, directly over the small platform where Roberts was working. Roberts claimed that the counterweight actually struck him, forcing him down to the floor of the platform, and resulting in a serious injury. His lawsuit was *David Roberts v. Hoechst Celanese Corporation*. I represented the defendant, Hoechst Celanese Corporation. The principle issues were whether or not the counterweight actually struck Roberts, and even if it did strike him, the severity of the injury. It was strongly suspected that his injury was minimal, and perhaps non-existent.

Roberts lived in Port Arthur, Texas, and his attorney was also in Port Arthur. The plaintiff's deposition was scheduled in his attorney's office in Port Arthur. I was taken aback when Roberts entered the conference room at the beginning of the deposition; he walked with a cane, stooped over, taking small, shuffling steps, and grimacing with each step, as if each step produced pain. He claimed that the accident had rendered him permanently crippled and disabled. We strongly suspected that Roberts was exaggerating his injury and was malingering. We decided that this was a case which called for covert surveillance.

The decision to engage an investigator to conduct surveillance and surreptitiously photograph a party is not an easy one. While it sometimes can produce dramatic results, it can also back-fire. If the investigator takes pictures which corroborate the plaintiff's claims, the pictures may be discoverable by the plaintiff. If so, you have provided the plaintiff strong evidence for his case. On the other hand, if the pictures or video evidence contradict the plaintiff's claims, they can be very persuasive. The decision to conduct surveillance is somewhat of a gamble.

In this case, the results were dramatic. Our investigator obtained video images of David Roberts mowing his lawn without any indication of impairment or difficulty. He was photographed jogging in his neighborhood. The videotape of Roberts jogging and mowing his lawn was in sharp contrast to his testimony and his appearance when his deposition was taken. This was powerful evidence that he was malingering and exaggerating his injury.

Prior to trial, the court ordered the parties to conduct mediation. The mediator was Tommy Proctor, an excellent and very experienced mediator. But the mediation stalled. The parties were not close to an agreement, and it appeared that we were headed for an impasse. The plaintiff's attorney was unaware that we had a videotape of his client which could absolutely destroy his client's claims of a serious injury. Thus, we had to make another difficult decision: do we save the damaging videotape for trial, and ambush the plaintiff's attorney, or do we disclose it now, in an effort to convince the plaintiff's attorney of the weakness of his case?

We decided upon the safer course of action - to disclose it during the mediation session, thinking that the plaintiff, after viewing the tape, would reduce his settlement demand to a sum that would enable us to settle the case. So, the mediator convened both parties into his conference room for the showing of the dramatic videotape. Not a word was spoken as the tape was being played. You could have heard a pin drop. I watched Roberts and his attorney carefully as the tape concluded, and they exited the conference room. The attorney appeared to be in shock. He had just seen images which completely decimated his case. Roberts himself never changed his expression - he appeared to be unmoved by the showing of the videotape. Then, as he walked out the door, he announced "That's not me, that's my brother". We (my client's general counsel, Ben Ramsey and I) were dumbfounded; was it possible that our investigator had made a mistake and had photographed the wrong person? The house in the videotape was clearly Roberts' house. The jogging was clearly in Roberts' neighborhood. We pored over the images - it appeared to be Roberts, but we had to admit that we could not say for sure that the person in the videotape was Roberts. We left with the very disquieting possibility that our surveillance had back-fired. We had now disclosed the tape to the plaintiff's attorney, and he would undoubtedly use it at trial to show the jury that we had surreptitiously photographed someone other than David Roberts. The jury would not have been amused.

Still not sure who the person in the videotape was, I called the plaintiff's attorney, and asked him to make Roberts' brother available for his deposition. He said he would. But time passed, and the trial date was getting closer, and I had not heard from him. I asked for an address for the brother, so I could subpoena him. No response. We filed a motion with the court, asking that the location of the plaintiff's brother be disclosed so that we could take his deposition. Still no response. We got one excuse after another. He was on vacation, out of town, was ill, and unable to be deposed, his address was unknown, etc. It was becoming clear that we were never going to get a straight answer about the brother's whereabouts.

Finally, shortly before our motion before the court was to be heard, the plaintiff's attorney called me. He sounded dejected, as if he were on his last leg. There was no brother! The person in the video was David Roberts!

Not surprisingly, the case settled for the sum that we had originally offered.

O Brother, Where Art Thou?

CHAPTER 12

THE CASE ON THE LAW SCHOOL
FINAL EXAM

*A*daway v. *Delta Foremost Chemical Corporation* was tried in Federal District Court in Beaumont. The Honorable Robert Parker was the trial judge. I was well acquainted with Judge Parker. Before being appointed to the bench, he practiced law in Longview, and I had practiced there as well. In fact, I tried a case against him in federal court in Marshall. In the *Adaway* case, I represented Delta Foremost Chemical Corporation, located in Memphis, Tennessee. Delta Foremost is a manufacturer and distributer of various chemical products, primarily to the hospitality industry. There were about 20 to 30 plaintiffs in the case. The lead plaintiff was a restaurant in Port Arthur, Bobby's Fish House and Oyster Bar, and its owner.

My client sold various chemicals and cleaning agents in large drums. Bobby's Fish House and Oyster Bar was a customer. The restaurant ordered two drums from my client, a drum of grill cleaner, and a drum of insecticide. Upon arrival, the two drums were placed in the restaurant's storage area, side by side. An employee set out to clean the grill in the kitchen. He made a rather serious mistake, however, because he used the insecticide instead of the grill cleaner! At least that was our contention. The plaintiffs claimed that the drums were mislabeled. Unfortunately, the drums and their contents had been disposed of prior to the filing of the suit, so that issue was never completely resolved. There were a number of customers in the restaurant at the time. Allegedly, everybody in the restaurant became ill. The restaurant closed, and never re-opened. Ironically, all of the plaintiffs sought treatment from the same local doctor.

Frank Mitchell was a law student at Baylor Law School, and worked for our firm as a briefing clerk during the summer. Frank had worked on the case, and had researched several legal issues in connection with it. At the end of the summer, Frank returned to law school. He worked for us again the next summer. By this time, the case had been tried. Actually, it was settled during trial. One day, Frank casually mentioned to me that "my case" had been on his final examination in Torts. I couldn't imagine what he was talking about. He said "Yes, your case, the one about the restaurant that went out of business after the grill was cleaned with insecticide, and a lot of people got sick." He went on to say that his final examination in Torts was an essay exam, and the fact situation in the *Adaway* case was on the test. The students were asked to identify the legal issues in the case, and discuss each issue, including how each issue should be resolved. As you would expect, Frank made the high "A" on the exam. I still could not imagine how the fact situation in the case had found its way to the final exam in Torts at Baylor. After digging in to the mystery, I learned that the professor had read about the case in a Beaumont newspaper, and had decided that the facts of the case would make a great exam question, because of the many legal issues that were presented.

CHAPTER 13

TRUTH: THE DEFENSE
TO A CLAIM OF SLANDER

In the early 80's, the medical procedure known as percutaneous transluminal coronary angioplasty (PTCA), usually referred to as "angioplasty" was in its infancy. PTCA or angioplasty is an invasive procedure to open blocked coronary arteries, allowing blood to circulate unobstructed to the heart. It utilizes a balloon catheter which is inserted into an artery - usually in the groin - but sometimes in the arm or wrist, and guided into a coronary artery where there is a blockage, and inflated to open the artery. The development of the procedure literally revolutionized the medical specialty of cardiology. Some cardiologists rushed to obtain the necessary training to become qualified and proficient in the procedure. It was also a gold mine, financially, for those cardiologists who were qualified early on. Dr. Maidi Al-Boustani was one of those.

Dr. Al-Boustani recognized very early the benefits of becoming qualified in the procedure. He received his training, and developed a thriving practice resulting from referrals from other cardiologists. But there were some who questioned whether he was moving too fast, and whether he was performing some unnecessary procedures. He applied to a number of hospitals for privileges so that he could perform procedures at those hospitals, and encountered some opposition at several of the hospitals to which he applied. He eventually brought suit against three physicians for slander, alleging that they had made defamatory statements about him in various peer committee meetings, and had damaged his reputation, resulting in his loss of income, for all of which he sought millions in damages. The case was *Al-Boustani v. Guttin, et al.* It was filed in the 215th Judicial Court of Harris County, Texas. The judge was the Honorable Eugene Chambers, a rather surly old judge who had been the law librarian at the Harris County Courthouse before being elected district judge. My client was Daniel Freeman, a young cardiologist who practiced primarily at Memorial Hospital Southwest. The other two defendants were Dr. Jorge (George) Guttin, and Dr. Robert Hall. Guttin was represented by Charlie Parker, a brilliant and skilled young lawyer, and Dr. Hall was represented by Charles Boston of Fulbright and Jaworski, a renowned trial lawyer. Dr. Guttin practiced primarily at Memorial Hospital Southeast, and Dr. Hall was chief of cardiology at The Methodist Hospital in the Texas Medical Center.

The trial of the case was a stressful undertaking for everyone involved. The stakes were high, and medical careers were on the line. Nevertheless, there were some light moments. Judge Chambers appeared to doze on the bench from time to time. Several days into the trial, he was leaning back in his chair, when the chair overturned, and the judge ended up on the floor. He scrambled to his feet and simply said "Carry on".

On another occasion, Dr. Al-Boustani was on the witness stand being questioned on direct examination by his attorney. Dr. Al-Boustani was a native of Iraq. His attorney, in tracing his immigration to the United States, asked him how he was able to leave Iraq. Dr. Al-Boustani turned toward the jury and said, through clenched teeth and with a heavy accent, "I swam the Tigris River". Whereupon, Dr. Guttin, a native of Mexico, leaned over the counsel table and said to his attorney, but probably loud enough for the jury to hear, "I also swam a river to get here".

On still another occasion Dr. Guttin was on the witness stand with a stack of exhibits and other documents in front of him. His attorney, Charlie Parker, asked him to look at a particular document. Dr. Guttin was frantically looking through the stack of documents, but could not locate the document he was asked to look at. Finally, Charlie realized that Dr. Guttin did not have the requested document, but it was on the counsel table in front of Charlie, who then said "Never mind, Dr. Guttin, I have the document". Dr. Guttin then turned toward the jury, looking exasperated, and said "My lawyer is against me". That broke up the jury, and lightened the mood in the courtroom. Dr. Guttin had a wonderful sense of humor, and a great sense of timing. His sense of humor kept us all somewhat relaxed in an otherwise stressful situation.

Dr. Richard Kones, the notorious perpetrator of Medicare and billing fraud was a potential witness in the case. Dr. Kones was a brilliant and promising young cardiologist, but he was also a convicted felon. He had been convicted of billing and Medicare fraud for billing for non-existent procedures. The attorneys in the case traveled to upstate New York, where Kones was incarcerated, to take his deposition. After being released from prison, he moved to Philadelphia and began practice there, but was again arrested, charged and convicted of billing fraud. This was Kones' 6th conviction for submitting false billings to medical insurance carriers.

Dr. Robert Hall was Chief of Cardiology at Methodist Hospital in Houston. He had been President Dwight Eisenhower's personal physician and had been Chief of Cardiology at Walter Reed Hospital in Washington, D. C. He was retired from the military after 21 years, and had received the Legion of Merit and the "A" Prefix in Cardiology, the highest award for professional accomplishment within the Army. He had been persuaded to come to Houston after his retirement from the Army by Dr. Denton Cooley, who founded the Texas Heart Institute and who performed the first successful heart transplant in the United States. When he was called to testify, and Charles Boston led him through his accomplishments, his awards, and through each phase of his storied career, the case was virtually over as to him. The plaintiff's attorney never asked him a question. I'm not sure I have ever seen a witness with a more commanding presence than Dr. Hall.

Charles Boston, anticipating a quick defense verdict, invited all the defendants' attorneys and the defendants and their spouses to a "victory" dinner at the Houston Racquet Club on the evening of the first day of jury deliberation. The only trouble was that the jury did not come back with a quick verdict. On the evening of the dinner, the jury was still out. It was a very awkward evening. We were not in a festive mood. Rather, it was a very stressful and depressing evening. Conventional wisdom says that a quick verdict is usually a defendant's verdict; the longer the jury stays out, the more likely the chances of a plaintiff's verdict. And our jury deliberated for an uncomfortably long time. Our concern turned to elation, however, on the next day when the jury returned a verdict for all three defendants.

CHAPTER 14

A POPULAR PLAINTIFF

It was a busy Friday afternoon in Wharton, Texas. Dell Young, wife of Perry Young, a prominent and well-liked local attorney, was driving home on a busy two-lane roadway. Edward Orsak was traveling in the opposite direction on the same roadway, pulling a trailer. His trailer hitch was old, rusted, and in poor condition. As the two vehicles approached one another, the old trailer hitch failed, the trailer separated from the pulling vehicle, crossed the center stripe, and struck Dell Young's vehicle head-on. The EMTs arrived shortly, and Mrs. Young was transported to the small hospital in Wharton. She was x-rayed and examined by an emergency room physician on duty, and released. Tylenol was prescribed for her pain. Over the course of the week-end, her condition deteriorated. She complained of pain in her back and in her chest. She was increasingly restless. Her daughter stayed with her on Saturday, and had to help her walk to the bathroom. She had a massive bruise on her left shoulder. On Sunday, she seemed to be slow to respond. On Monday morning, Perry Young took his wife back to the hospital in Wharton, and she was admitted. By Tuesday morning, she was unable to immediately recognize her family members. The decision was made to transport her by

Life-Flight to Methodist Hospital in the Texas Medical Center in Houston. Her condition continued to deteriorate, and she passed away approximately three weeks later. Her death was a slow and painful one.

Perry Young, Dell's surviving husband, and her children filed suit in the 329th District Court of Wharton County, Texas. The suit was styled *L. Perry Young, et al v. Edward Orsak, et al.* My client in the case was the Scott Fetzer Company, the manufacturer of the trailer hitch. The overriding issue in the case was the cause of death. The plaintiffs would contend that the cause of Dell's death was the trauma she sustained in the automobile accident. The defendants' contention was that alcohol and Tylenol, and their consumption immediately following the accident, resulted in liver failure, and ultimately, her death. The expert who testified on behalf of the defendants was Dr. Wayne Snodgrass, who was a professor of pharmacology and toxicology at the University of Texas Medical Branch in Galveston. Dell Young's pre-accident medical records were replete with references to her alcohol abuse and Tylenol abuse.

We knew that Perry Young's standing in the community, and his popularity, would be a factor in the case. He was very well-liked, and we knew that it might be difficult to select a jury which was not biased in his favor. But we were not prepared for what we found as we arrived in the courtroom on the Monday morning when the case was set for trial. The entire Wharton County Bar Association was seated behind the plaintiff's counsel table! Their presence occupied about half of the courtroom. It was an extremely effective demonstration of support for one of their own. If we did not already realize what we were up against, it became very clear at that time.

Rachel Bahnsen, the daughter of Perry and Dell Young, was a law student at South Texas School of Law at the time of the trial. She was probably the most credible and effective witness at the trial. A very articulate and impressive young woman, she strongly disputed the claims of her mother's alcohol and Tylenol abuse, in spite of the fact that the medical records so indicated. The following excerpts are from her direct examination by her attorney, Gary Stephens:

Q: Tell us who you are, please.
A: Rachel Bahnsen.
Q: And Mrs. Bahnsen, are you related to Perry and Dell Young?
A: Yes, I'm their daughter.
Q: You grew up in Wharton?
A: Yes.
Q: Are you proud to be Perry and Dell's daughter?
A: I couldn't have asked for better parents.
Q: You know we're here to talk about your mother's death?
A: Yes, sir.

Q: You've heard part of the testimony in this case that suggests that your mother abused drugs. Did you ever see any indication of that?
A: Never.
Q: Did you ever see any indication that your mother would take a whole great big handful of Tylenol?
A: Never. My mother was an intelligent woman.
Q: Ever see any indication that she was abusing alcohol?
A: No, sir. I don't know why anyone, when she's not here, would go and try to do a character assassination on my mother. And I'm here to tell you they're not true because no one knew her like I did, nobody. Not a person in this courtroom, not anyone else that could come in here.
Q: How does that make you feel about those allegations about her?

A: It's shame, anger, frustration; she was part of me and to be attacked and to be lied about is the worst thing you can do. She would have never done that to anybody else. She taught us not to do that. And I just expected that nobody else would do it, but I was wrong.

Q: I'm going to ask you one question about alcohol because I don't really think it's in the case, but did you see any indication of any alcohol use or abuse or the presence of alcohol or the use of alcohol by your mother during that period of time we're talking about, the date of the wreck, the 28th, and for the rest of her life?
A: Absolutely not. That is the most ludicrous thing anyone could come in here and say, and I have no idea where anyone could get that idea. I sat with her. I held her. I took care of her. It's a lie.

Q: Now, you heard this testimony about that being delirium tremens and that being attributable to the alcohol withdrawal.

MR. CHANDLER: Object to the form of the question.

THE COURT: Sustained.

Q: (By Mr. Stephens) You've heard some testimony about delirium tremens; is that right?
A: Yes, sir.

Q: And you've heard some testimony that your mother experienced that sort of a state?
A: Yes, sir.

Of course she went on to testify as to how her mother's death had
affected her, and her testimony was powerful. She was truly a
sympathetic witness. It is dangerous for a lawyer to cross-examine such a witness. If the jury perceives that the cross-examiner
has been unfair or rude or confrontational to the witness, it may
hold it against that lawyer, and his client. In fact, the other defense
counsel chose not to ask Rachel a single question. But Rachel had
suggested in her direct examination that the defendants were making up the evidence about Dell's alcohol and Tylenol abuse, when,
in fact, that information came from Dell's medical records, which
the defendants had nothing to do with. I felt I had to challenge
her accusations that the defendants were lying and manufactur-
ing evidence, but I knew I had to do so in a gentle, respectful, and
forthright manner. At the conclusion of her direct examination,
the following occurred.

MR. STEPHENS: Pass the witness.
THE COURT: Mr. Chandler?
MR: CHANDLER: I don't have any questions.
MR. BOANERGES: No questions.
MR. FUNDERBURK: Just a couple, Your Honor, if I may.

CROSS-EXAMINATION
QUESTIONS BY MR. FUNDERBURK:

Q: Rachel, I want to tell you before I ask you a single question that I respect your feelings and what you're going
   through here today and your feelings about the issues in
   this case, all right?
A: Thank you.

Q: Now, let me ask you this, Rachel, you're an intelligent woman; you have two degrees; you're in law school now, right?

A: Yes.

Q: You know you're going to be a lawyer, that's what you intend to do?

A: Yes, sir.

Q: And you know because of that, that a lawyer is an officer of the court?

A: Yes, sir.

Q: Rachel, you know that whenever a lawsuit is filed as your family has done in this case, that the plaintiff when he files the lawsuit puts in issue all the essential elements of the cause of action. You understand that, don't you?

A: Yes.

Q: And you know that when that was done in this case, that the cause of death, the cause of your mother's death was an issue that became an issue at that time. You know that?

A: Yes, sir.

Q: Now, Rachel, are you suggesting in any way that any of these lawyers for the defense have invented something for this lawsuit?

A: I'm not suggesting they invented anything. I'm saying what is being said in here is not true.

Q: Well, have you read all the medical records?

A: No, sir.

Q: Okay. But you know that from what you've heard in the courtroom here today and yesterday, you know that the medical records, the medical tests, the blood tests, the autopsy, these are things that were done by physicians both here in Wharton and at Methodist Hospital in Houston at the time of your mother's illness. You know that?

A: Yes.

Q: And regardless of what anybody believes or wants to believe about the case, these are scientific facts involved.
You know that?

A: They're in the record.

⇌ ⇌

Q: All right. Thank you, Rachel. That's all I have.

A: You're welcome.

After several days of trial, the case was settled on very favorable
terms.

CHAPTER 15

THE JURY VISITS THE SCENE OF
THE ACCIDENT

Larry York and I were close friends. He was from Palestine, as was I. I had known him since childhood. Larry had just begun his practice with the firm of Baker and Botts. We found ourselves on opposite sides of a small case in Judge Jack Treadway's Justice of the Peace court, in the old criminal courts building. The case involved a fender-bender, which occurred in downtown Houston, just a couple of blocks from the courthouse. It was the shortest jury case I ever tried. Larry York represented the defendant, and I represented the plaintiff. We started the trial at 9:00 a.m. I called one witness, who gave his account of how the accident happened, and rested my case. Larry called his client as a witness, and rested. Both sides rested by 10:00 a.m. We were given 10 minutes each for closing argument, and the arguments were completed by 10:30 a.m. The jury retired to the jury room to consider their verdict. At 12:00 noon the jury had not reached its verdict. Judge Treadway called the jury into open court, and inquired as to the jury's progress. The foreman of the six person jury stated that they were hopelessly deadlocked, five to one (In the mid-sixties, when this case was tried, the verdict had to be unanimous; that is no longer the case). Judge Treadway recessed the case for lunch; the jury was told to report back to the courtroom at 2:00 p.m. and resume deliberations. They did so. Within five minutes, the buzzer sounded, the signal that the jury had reached a verdict. Judge Treadway called the jury into open court. The foreman announced a verdict for the plaintiff, my client. Apparently, the juror who had been the hold-out had changed his vote. The judge accepted the verdict, and discharged the jury. As we were leaving the courtroom, Larry York and I entered the elevator with several of the jurors. We asked the jurors on the elevator what had changed the mind of the hold-out juror. One juror answered "I was the hold-out before lunch, but during the lunch recess, we all walked over to the intersection where the accident occurred, and the other jurors pointed out to me how the accident could not have happened the way I thought it happened. So, I changed my vote". Larry and I just shook our heads; he was clearly entitled to a new trial as a result of the jury's unauthorized visit to the accident scene. Thankfully, his client elected not to pursue a new trial. Jurors sometimes do strange things!

CHAPTER 16

SEMPER FIDELIS

The three years I spent as a Marine Corps lawyer were invaluable in my development as a trial lawyer. At that time, the Marine Corps did not have a Judge Advocate General Corps, as the other branches of the military had. All Marine lawyers were line offices first, meaning that his or her training was no different than that of an infantry officer. Officers Basic School in Quantico Virginia was a six-month school, very much like "boot camp" for enlisted personnel, but with added classroom instruction. Upon graduation from Basic School, a military occupational specialty (MOS) was assigned to each graduate. My MOS was trial/defense counsel. At that time, I received orders to Naval Justice School in Newport, Rhode Island, a six-week school on the Uniform Code of Military Justice (UCMJ). From there, I was assigned to the Division Legal Office, 1st Marine Division, Camp Pendleton, California. The high point in Basic School, for me, was being appointed President of the Mess, a formal dinner, called Mess Night, shortly prior to graduation, honoring those Marines who have gone before, and the traditions of the Marine Corps. The speaker for the occasion was a Marine general. The President of the Mess is more or less the master of ceremonies.

I reported to Camp Pendleton, California on the day that President Kennedy was assassinated, November 22, 1963. I was immediately assigned duties as defense counsel for both general and special courts-martial. I represented Marines accused of various crimes and UCMJ violations. One of those cases stands out in my mind. The case was *U. S. v. Unger.* Lance Corporal Robert Unger was stationed at Twenty-nine Palms, California, a Marine base in the desert of Southern California, approximately 150 miles from Camp Pendleton. He was from Los Angeles, and came from a very well-to-do family. He and another Marine allegedly broke into the base armory one night, and stole a large cache of various weapons. They were quickly apprehended and charged with breaking and entering, and theft. I made several trips from Camp Pendleton to Twenty-nine Palms to meet with Unger, who was in the brig, and to investigate the case. Just prior to trial, Unger's father hired a well-known criminal lawyer from Chicago, Robert C. Buckley, to assist me in the trial of the case. I was quite happy to turn lead counsel responsibilities over to him. I was able to assist Buckley, and I learned a lot from a seasoned trial lawyer during the trial. Nevertheless, Unger was convicted. Each evening during the trial, Buckley and I drove from Twenty-nine Palms to Palm Springs for dinner, a distance of about 50 miles. Buckley believed in living in style, since he was being paid handsomely for his representation of Unger by Unger's father. I was treated to luxuries to which a young Marine Lieutenant was unaccustomed. Dining in Palm Springs was a lot different from the evening mess hall fare on the base. Buckley was a great lawyer, and a wonderful gentleman. After the trial, he sent me an engraved memento with the inscription *U.S. v. Unger.*

CHAPTER 17

U.S. V. DUNBAR

O ne of the Marines I was assigned to represent was Corporal Larry Dunbar. I confess that I had forgotten about his case, when, in 2010, I received the following letter from him, which stirred my memory:

Feb. 1, 2010
Mr. Larry Funderburk
This past week I was thinking of an incident that changed my life, and your name came to mind. I never imagined I would be able to locate you, but with Google all things are possible.
In 1964 I was a Corporal (E-4) in the Marine Corps. I was three years into a four year enlistment when I did a very stupid thing. I, along with another Marine stole a transmission out of a Corvette that had been repossessed by the credit union on base. Our intention was to install it in a drag car we were building. Obviously we were not very adept at stealing and we were arrested by the authorities. We were to be tried before a general court-martial. This is where you come into the picture. When I contacted the legal department, you were assigned to represent me. The first thing you did was to get the charges lowered and I was tried at a

special court-martial. You spent a lot of time explaining the legal process and preparing my defense. As I think back to that time I realize how fortunate I was to be represented by you. You showed a lot of compassion, dedication, and put forth the effort necessary to provide me with the best possible outcome. As a direct result of your diligence, I received an honorable discharge and in effect started civilian life with a clean slate.

After the verdict was read at my trial, I don't remember thanking you. So that is really the motive behind my writing this letter. Forty-six years after the fact I do want to say thank you. I've never had any more brushes with the law since that terrible incident. I married the girl I was dating while in the service. We celebrated our 45th anniversary this past November.

Again, thank you for helping me during the darkest time of my life. May God bless you.

Sincerely,

/s/

Larry Dunbar

CHAPTER 18

TRIAL BY FIRE

I n the fall of 1964 I was transferred to 3rd Marine Division legal office on Okinawa. I continued to act as both trial counsel (prosecutor) and defense counsel. The more experience I gained, the greater my case load grew. In March of 1965, the first American combat troops landed in Viet Nam. They were part of the 3rd Marine Division. In May of 1965, I received my orders to Viet Nam, and spent the rest of that year there. The Division headquarters was at Da Nang. The 4th Marine Regiment, however, was assigned to provide security for a Naval airfield at Chu Lai, located about sixty miles south of Da Nang. I was assigned the additional duty of Legal Officer for the 4th Marine Regiment. This meant that I split my time between Da Nang and Chu Lai. Our quarters in Da Nang were an old French army compound. But at least we had a roof over our heads. In Chu Lai, we lived in tents and the legal office was in a tent. Practicing law in this environment was challenging, to say the least. We endured the monsoon rains, mud and dust. Mildew quickly formed on any stationary object. Passing vehicles left clouds of dust in their wake. It rained incessantly during the monsoon season. We had virtually no law library. Although we had access to Vietnamese translators, Da Nang was on a border area for local dialects and it was difficult to find a translator who could communicate with witnesses. In addition, there was a cultural gap which seemed to result in the Vietnamese witnesses trying to testify to whatever they thought we wanted to hear. We had significant translation problems. Also, locating and interviewing witnesses was extremely difficult, both Vietnamese witnesses and Marine witnesses. Vietnamese witnesses could seemingly disappear into the countryside and the small villages. Locating witnesses was dangerous. You never knew for sure who the enemy was. Many of the local citizenry were ordinary farmers by day, but Viet Cong by night. To an American, Vietnamese names were similar and confusing. Phone books and subpoenas were not an option. There was simply no practical way to require a Vietnamese witness to appear at trial. As for Marine witnesses, if he was an infantryman, he was probably on patrol or in the field. It might be difficult to even locate his company, since the companies moved often. Or he might be on R & R leave, or have rotated back to the U. S. Or he might have been killed or wounded. In spite of these challenges, we prosecuted and defended many cases. We had a high volume of negligent homicide cases in which Marines mishandled their weapons with tragic consequences. Sleeping on post was a frequent offense. Serious offenses such as homicide, rape, and robbery were tried.

CHAPTER 19

U. S. V. MCGHEE

Lance Corporal Marion McGhee was a fireteam leader in his company, located on the Chu Lai perimeter. He had no record of disciplinary violations. Several of his fellow Marines noted that his behavior on the occasion in question seemed unusual. Some testified that he seemed to be drunk; others testified that his behavior was "strange", but he didn't appear to be drunk. Around 9:00 p.m. on the evening in question, McGhee walked through the Marine lines, past the defensive barbed wire and toward a nearby village. He was challenged by a Marine sentry, but responded that he was going after a Viet Cong. Two Marines were dispatched to bring him back to his company. As they approached the village, they heard a shot and a woman's scream and then saw McGhee walking toward them, leaving the village. In a calm voice, he stated that he had just killed a VC and that he was being followed by more VC. Then he announced that he was going to get the VC following him, and started back toward the village, despite the efforts of his fellow Marines to stop him. Within a few minutes, he returned to his company, with a "wild look", according to one witness.

At his trial, Vietnamese prosecution witnesses testified that McGhee had kicked through the wall of the hut where a family slept. He seized a 14-year-old girl and pulled her toward the door. When her father interceded, McGhee shot and killed him. Once outside the house, the girl was able to escape with the help of her grandmother.

McGhee was, of course, charged with first degree murder, and ordered to stand trial before a general court-martial. Lieutenant (USN) Don Campbell and I were appointed to represent him. He continued to assert that he was pursuing someone whom he suspected was a VC. Our defense was insanity.

I vividly remember the difficulty we encountered in identifying witnesses, both Vietnamese and Marines, and securing their testimony. The language barrier was another huge problem. We had great difficulty making the witnesses understand our questions, even with the help of a Vietnamese translator. The trial took place in a tent in Da Nang.

After lengthy testimony by two psychiatrists, the court concluded that the prosecution had met its burden of proof, and that McGhee was free from mental defect, disease, or derangement and was able to distinguish right from wrong, and adhere to the right, beyond a reasonable doubt. He was found guilty of unpremeditated murder, and sentenced to reduction to private, loss of all pay and allowances, confinement at hard labor for ten years, and a dishonorable discharge. On appeal, his confinement was reduced to seven years. He actually served six years and one month.

Lance Corporal McGhee was the first Marine to be convicted of the murder of a Vietnamese non-combatant. Indeed, this was the first murder case to be tried in Vietnam, wherein an American combatant was the accused.

Lieutenant (USN) Don Campbell and I served together both on Okinawa and in Vietnam. He was a great friend and a brilliant lawyer. He made a career of the Navy, achieving the rank of Rear Admiral. In 1986, he was appointed Judge Advocate General of the Navy, the highest ranking lawyer in the Navy.

As an aside, Don suffered a debilitating stroke several years after his retirement from the Navy, which left him unable to speak clearly. I received a telephone call one morning in my office, but the voice on the other end was unintelligible. I could not understand what the person was saying. I was inclined to simply hang up, concluding that the caller was drunk, or perhaps had the wrong number. But something told me that this was someone I knew, and that I should not dismiss this call so quickly. After several minutes listening to the caller slurring his speech in an unintelligible manner, and not recognizing the caller, he began to hum The Marine Corps Hymn. I immediately knew who it was! It was Don Campbell!

CHAPTER 20

THE WESTCHASE HILTON FIRE

The Westchase Hilton Hotel, in southwest Houston, erupted in flames at 2:00 a.m. on March 7, 1982. Twelve people lost their lives. Numerous lawsuits were filed and consolidated. I represented Britain Electric Co., the electrical contractor for the hotel when it was built. Legendary trial lawyer Joe Jamail represented a husband whose wife died as the result of smoke inhalation. The husband and his wife had crawled down the hall through the smoke, but he lost her in the smoke. All of the fatalities were smoke related. Numerous defendants were named in the various lawsuits which were filed, including the Westchase Hilton hotel and the fire alarm contractor. Mike Terry, an attorney with the firm of Vinson and Elkins, represented the hotel. The staff that had been on duty that night was interviewed the next day. It was learned that the clerk manning the desk received a fire alarm signal from the 8th floor around 2:00 a.m. He also received a call from a guest on that floor. He turned the alarm off, and dispatched a security guard to investigate. While the security guard was on his way to investigate, the alarm from the 8th floor sounded again. The clerk turned off the alarm again. The guard took the service elevator to the 8th floor, and found a woman standing outside her room complaining of smoke in her room. He went in to investigate. There was no fire in the room, but there was smoke coming in from the bathroom exhaust vent. He determined that the source of the smoke was on a floor below. He went back to the service elevator and descended floor by floor. Upon reaching the 4th floor, he found it completely enveloped in thick smoke. He notified the front desk. The desk clerk called the fire department and sounded the general alarm. It was 2:25 a.m. Ten people were probably already dead. Five were seriously injured, and two more died later. A family of four and a family of five were found in rooms 407 and 411. One man died in the hallway, apparently turning away from the stairwell and into a *cul de sac* in response to a confusing "EXIT" sign. The tragedy was almost unspeakable!

It was eventually determined that the source of the smoke was a fire in a single room on the 4th floor, occupied by a Hilton employee from out of town. It was theorized that he had left a smoldering cigarette in a chair in his room, left and returned later to find his room fully involved in smoke. The fresh air which entered the room when he opened the door caused the room to burst into flame. He left the room, but did not fully close the door, and the door stayed open; it did not fully close on its own. The fire raged in that room. There was heat damage to the rooms on either side. The corridor of the 4th floor was filled with thick smoke. All of the deaths and injuries were caused by smoke inhalation.

If the source of the fire was on the 4th floor, why did the alarm come in from the 8th floor? It was discovered that there were no smoke sensors in the individual rooms; the sensors were located in the corridor and in the elevator lobby. Therefore the smoke had to get out of the room and into the corridor before the smoke would be detected and the alarm would sound. There were vertical chases in the hotel so that all the bathrooms were stacked vertically and shared a common exhaust chase. Smoke from a room, therefore, would travel vertically. It appeared that is what happened on the night of the fire. Smoke traveled vertically to the room on the 8th floor. The guest in that room returned to her room, opened her door, and allowed the smoke to drift to the sensor in the corridor, causing the alarm on that floor to sound. By the time the source of the smoke was discovered, it was too late.

There were other problems which contributed to the tragedy as well. The door to the guest room on the 4th floor should have closed on its own. The hotel design called for self-closing doors to protect the guest. However, the contractor did not fully correct a punch list item at construction that noted some doors did not close because the bottom of the door dragged on the carpet. The building contractor apparently did not rehang those doors to allow for self-closing.

It was also learned that during construction, automatic sprinklers were considered, but rejected in order "to reduce cost."

For all these reasons, and others, the hotel accepted liability, but sought contribution from the other defendants.

Mike Terry, the attorney for the hotel was overwhelmed by the publicity, the media attention and the feeding frenzy that followed one dramatic admission after another. Rumors abounded; *"the clerk shut off the alarm.......the live-in manager attempted to order a helicopter to the roof of the hotel to evacuate him and his family......."*etc. Mike Terry was deeply shaken by the weight of his representation of the hotel and his contemplation of the individual deaths and the unspeakable horror of the probable last moments of people who were simply sound asleep in a modern hotel when this tragic chain of events unfolded.

OUTTAKES

I t has often been said that only 5% or less of all cases filed actually go to trial. To put it another way, 95% or more of all civil lawsuits filed are either settled or resolved in some manner prior to trial. I believe this to be true. I know it was true in my own practice. My best estimate is that in my 50+ years of practice, I actually handled more than 3,000 cases. It would be impossible to recall the details of so many cases, but a few memories remain.

On December 27, 1977, the Bunge grain elevators in Galveston exploded. Twenty people lost their lives in the explosion. In the litigation which ensued, I represented Relco, Inc., the company which owned and operated the locomotive which was alleged to have been the ignition source for the explosion. Depositions were taken in San Francisco, Washington, D. C., Lincoln, Nebraska, New Orleans, and of course Houston and Galveston. I spent a lot of time with other lawyers who were representing different parties to the case. I had to get used to my client's locomotive being referred to as "old sparky".

I was taking the deposition of a plaintiff in a workers' compensation case. He had suffered a heart attack, and contended that his heart attack was caused by the conditions of his employment. My client, the insurer of the employer, denied that the employment had anything to do with the heart attack. I asked him, "When did you discover that your heart attack was caused by the conditions of your employment?" He replied, "When I went to see my lawyer!" Apparently, lawyers, as well as doctors, sometimes make medical diagnoses.

Ernest Cannon is an outstanding plaintiff's attorney, and one of the most feared and aggressive trial lawyers anywhere. He represented a young man who had received serious injuries in an automobile accident. The case was filed in Brazoria County. There were several defendants in the case. Cannon's settlement demand was $1.5 million. He knew that the defendants would eventually meet his demand, if he could get the case to trial. On the Monday morning when the case was set for trial, all the attorneys attended docket call before Judge J. Ray Gayle. After the docket was called, and the parties made their announcements of ready or not ready, Cannon's case was assigned the number two position for the week. It was thought to be unlikely that Judge Gayle would try more than one case that week. The number one case appeared to be a rather small automobile accident case. Ernest approached the attorney for the plaintiff in the first case and asked him what his settlement demand was. The attorney told him that he would settle his case for $10,000. Ernest replied "Settled!" That, of course, made his case the first case on the docket, and the trial was set to begin momentarily. Not surprisingly, his case settled as well. Ernest got the $1.5 million he knew he would get if he could get his case to trial.

While practicing in Longview, Texas, I tried several cases in Upshur County. Gilmer is the county seat. William Parker was a very successful plaintiff's lawyer there. He was also a very effective trial lawyer. He and the district clerk were close friends. He represented the plaintiffs in most of the personal injury cases in that county. We tried a case in which his client, a co-ed at the University of Texas, had received a back injury in an automobile accident. I had made a settlement offer, which he had turned down. His demand was more than twice the figure my client was willing to pay. So we proceeded to trial. When the jury retired to consider its verdict, William seemed to disappear. After a couple of hours, William emerged from a closet on the second floor of the courthouse, which normally was locked. He approached me, and said that his client had decided to accept my pre-trial offer. I soon learned the reason he capitulated and settled the case. It was apparently common knowledge around the courthouse that William was always given access to the closet, by the district clerk during jury deliberations. The closet was next to the jury room, with a very thin wall between. He could hear every word spoken in the jury room. The jury was about to render a verdict for the defendant! Access to the closet was the key to his success.

CONCLUSION

THE VANISHING JURY TRIAL

I cannot imagine any career which would have been more interesting and fulfilling than my career as a trial lawyer. It saddens me to see the gradual disappearance of the jury trial. I am sure there are many reasons for this. One explanation is the widespread use of mediation to resolve disputes, as well as other alternative dispute resolution strategies. I have participated in hundreds of mediations, and know from my own experience that mediation is an effective method with which to achieve resolution of a case. But mediation is basically a settlement conference in which the lawyers do most of the talking, and simply start out negotiating a settlement. No jury speeches, no cross-examination of witness, no jury selection, no framing of the issues in the court's charge, no sweating out a jury verdict, no rapid heart-beat when the buzzer sounds from the jury room, signaling a verdict, no working until mid-night during trial and every weekend during trial. In other words, no thrill of victory, no agony of defeat. The civil jury trial is all but extinct outside the United States, and we may be headed in that direction as well. We need the public to participate in our justice system by serving on juries, yet we seem to be headed in the opposite direction. The law schools continue to produce an abundance of extremely gifted, bright, young lawyers. Yet most of them will never have the privilege of trying a lawsuit before a jury, and experiencing the satisfaction of winning a hard-fought verdict from a jury. The cases are simply not available to be tried. What a tremendous privilege I have enjoyed, simply because I practiced in the golden age of trial work.

AUTHOR BIOGRAPHY

 Larry Funderburk joined the US Marines immediately after graduating from law school. A Vietnam veteran, he returned to practice civil trial law in Texas after being released from active duty. Though he is now semi- retired, in his fifty-year career, he took more than 150 cases to trial. From 2003 to 2016, he was named "Texas Super Lawyer" by *Texas Monthly* magazine. He received several awards from the Texas Association of Defense Counsel, as well as the Seventh Amendment award by the American Board of Trial Advocates.

41532394R00050

Made in the USA
Middletown, DE
17 March 2017